GRADE 2 SPELLING WORKBOOK: LEARN TO SPELL FOR KIDS

BABY PROFESSOR
EDUCATION KIDS

ANIMAL SPELLING

_ L L i G _ T _ _ _

BE___

C_T

D_NK_Y

_L_PH_NT

_L_Mi_G_

Gi___FFE

Hi__P__P__T__MUS

_GU_N_

J_GU___

K_NG_______

_i_N

M_C_W

N_W_

_ST_iCH

P _ G

QU_iL

_HiN_CE___S

S_EE_

_ i G E _

U_i_L

V__LE

W __ LF

X-___Y TET___

Y_K

Z__B____

ANSWERS

Alligator	Flamingo
Bear	Giraffe
Cat	Hippopotamus
Donkey	Iguana
Elephant	Jaguar

Kangaroo	Sheep
Lion	Tiger
Macaw	Urial
Newt	Vole
Ostrich	Wolf
Pig	X-ray Tetra
Quail	Yak
Rhinoceros	Zebra